Robert
Carrier
mini books

D1784292

978 0330 028561

Luncheon party menus

Contents

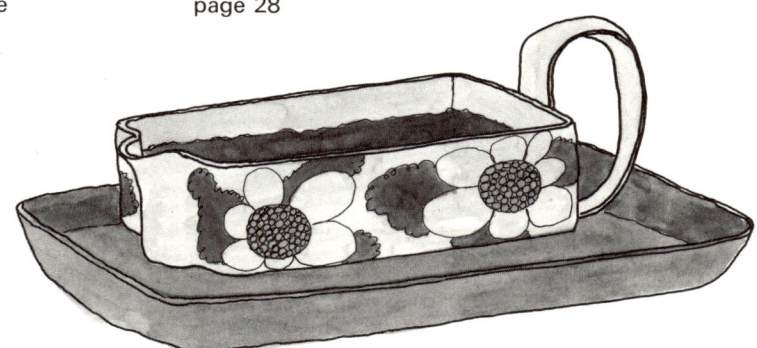

First published 1971 by
Pan Books Ltd
33 Tothill Street
London, S.W.1

Cover photo: *Informal weekend luncheon
parties are fun to give, fun to go to.*

© Robert Carrier 1971

Photographs by Angel Studio
Design and illustrations by
Artes Graphicae Ltd
Printed by the Cripplegate Printing Co. Ltd,
London, England

0 330 02856 1 Luncheon Party Menus

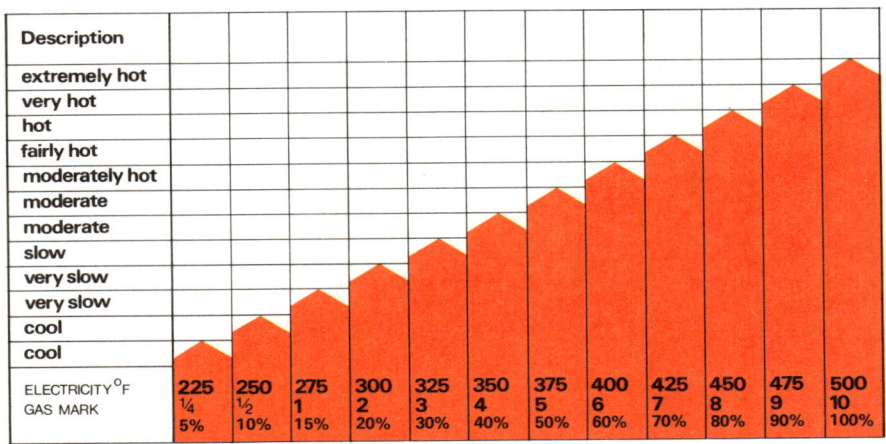

Description											
extremely hot											
very hot											
hot											
fairly hot											
moderately hot											
moderate											
moderate											
slow											
very slow											
very slow											
cool											
cool											
ELECTRICITY °F	225	250	275	300	325	350	375	400	425	450	475	500
GAS MARK	¼	½	1	2	3	4	5	6	7	8	9	10
	5%	10%	15%	20%	30%	40%	50%	60%	70%	80%	90%	100%

Oven Temperatures

All the recipes in this book were tested in both gas and electric ovens which adhered to the temperatures and gas settings above. If in doubt about your own oven, invest in an oven thermometer, which will also allow you to make spot checks in the future. Remember, though, to light the oven at least 15 to 20 minutes before taking a reading, and be prepared for a slight variance in temperature from top to bottom of oven.

How to follow a recipe successfully

■ **Read** recipe carefully through to the end. Calculate *total* preparation time, including hold-ups while marinating, chilling, etc.

■ **Make sure** you have all the necessary ingredients and utensils, and in the case of the latter, that they are of the correct size.

■ **Assemble** ingredients and utensils *before* you start. Remove eggs, butter, meat etc., from refrigerator in advance so that they will be at room temperature by the time you start to cook.

■ **Light** oven if a preheated oven is required. Set refrigerator to required setting if this is called for.

■ **Do** any advance preparation indicated in list of ingredients. The preparation of cake tins, etc., should also be attended to before you start.

■ **Measure** or weigh ingredients carefully.

■ **Do not** be tempted to alter a recipe in mid-stream until you have prepared it faithfully at least once, and do not telescope or ignore directions and procedures for combining ingredients unless you are a very experienced cook.

■ **Follow** cooking and/or baking times and temperatures given, but test for doneness about two-thirds of the way through or, conversely, be prepared to increase cooking time if it appears insufficient.

How to measure correctly

All spoon measurements in this book are level.
Accurate measurement is essential to any kind of cooking. A standard set of individual measuring spoons in plastic or metal—1 tablespoon,

1 teaspoon, $\frac{1}{2}$ teaspoon and $\frac{1}{4}$ teaspoon — is ideal for small quantities, and can be bought in many kitchen departments throughout the country. When a recipe calls for a fraction not catered for in the standard set, a dry ingredient can be measured by taking a whole spoonful, then carefully halving or quartering the amount with the tip of a knife and discarding the excess.

White Sugar: Make sure there are no lumps. Lift out a heaped spoonful and level off with a spatula or a straight knife.

Brown Sugar: Pack firmly into spoon so that when turned out, the sugar will hold the shape of the spoon. (*Note:* If brown sugar has hardened into a brick, leave it in the bread bin for a few hours to soften again.)

White Flour: Sift once. Dip spoon into flour, taking a heaped spoonful, and level off top with a spatula or a straight knife.

Other Flours/Fine Meals and Fine Crumbs: Stir instead of sifting. Measure like flour.

Baking Powder/Cream of Tartar/ Cornflour/Ground Herbs and Spices: Stir to loosen if necessary. Measure like flour.

Solid Fats: Soften fats before measuring. Then dip spoon into fat, scoop out, and level off top.

Syrup/Treacle/Liquid Honey: Dip spoon in hot water for 30 seconds before measuring to prevent syrup sticking to sides.

Larger Quantities

For measuring larger quantities of ingredients you will also need:

A Measuring Jug marked off in fluid ounces, and heatproof to withstand boiling liquids. You will also find this useful to use with American recipes, but remember that the American pint measures only 16 fluid ounces and the American cup or $\frac{1}{2}$ pint measures 8 fluid ounces.

Kitchen Scales. Select a pair with a large enough pan to hold the quantities you are likely to be measuring. You should be able to measure a pound of flour without spilling.

Luncheon Parties are Fun

■ Invite friends around for a meal and ten times out of ten they will assume that you mean dinner or supper.

■ Lunches seem to have been relegated to the realms of expense account living, or a quick "salad and coffee" on a shopping trip to town.

■ True, with husbands away from dawn till dusk, wives shopping frantically among the office lunch hour crowds or coping at home with endless snacks of baked beans, fish fingers or hamburgers as the children bundle in and out, there seems little place in our modern way of life for the leisurely late luncheon parties of our grandparents' day.

■ It helped, of course, in those days, to have a kitchenful of cooks and maids hard at work preparing the feast from the early morning.

■ You may think that weekday lunch parties in suburban deserts devoid of menfolk are a pleasure you can do without—but every week has its oasis, and it is then that the weekend luncheon with its comfortable pattern of unhurried food in a free-and-easy setting comes into its own.

■ What about those friends who live just that little bit too far away to make driving back after a late dinner party feasible? Ask them over for Sunday lunch instead. *You* can read the papers over coffee before you start putting the food together (especially if you've done some of the preparation the evening before), and *they* can still get back home in time to prepare themselves for the stark realities of Monday morning.

■ A weekend lunch party is a great idea for a group of friends who are planning to go on to some other activity together—be it a football match, a game of bridge, or just lazy chatter in the afternoon sun; for friends that you like well enough so you won't mind if they linger on into the evening (an occupational hazard for weekend lunch-party givers); or for friends with late-night baby-sitting problems (children are bright and relaxed enough early on in the day to enjoy you and your guests at the lunch table).

■ Some of my best lunch parties have been given in my house in the South of France.

■ There we can sit fourteen around the huge farmhouse table, and it's a sort of cook-as-you-eat pattern where guests help to string the beans and carry away the dishes as I produce the next course. Great fun.

■ Lunch parties *should* be informal. That's really why they are such a pleasure to go to or to give.

■ Don't treat a lunch party like a poor relation of a dinner party. For while the kind of food one serves is more or less elastic it is wise to keep it on the light side. And the drink as well. Save your heavier, more full-bodied wines for leisurely evenings when you can give yourself up to them fully without fear of the consequences.

■ Our menus for lunch parties are mainly three-course affairs—a light appetizer, a main course with a vegetable or salad, and an inspired sweet.

■ One of my favourite luncheon first courses—avocado, tomato and onion appetizer—was created when I myself was a weekend guest in the country and was asked to make something out of what was in the larder. To make it, peel avocado pears; cut them crosswise into thickish rings and combine them with thick slices of tomato and thin rings of onion; then toss in French dressing for a deliciously light luncheon appetizer.

■ The American version of an appetizer salad—Caesar Salad with Mushrooms—combines crisp leaves of Cos lettuce dressed with a cheese- and anchovy-flavoured dressing with garlic-scented croûtons and raw mushrooms.

■ Or try the recipe for *salade de moules au kari* (a fresh-tasting salad of curried mussels) or Crab Louis with Cucumber (tomato, cucumber and crab salad) to start your luncheon feast off with a flourish.

■ The main dishes in this book—sauté of veal with asparagus, roast chicken with almonds, little "tournedos" of lamb, and *omelette arlésienne*—all bring a note of lightness to the menus.

■ As do the sweets and puddings—pineapple ambrosia, cold lemon soufflé, blackcurrant sorbet, angel food cake, rhubarb pie and an orange-flavoured bread and butter pudding.

■ Get all the shopping done the day before—your three-course lunch will probably take up all of your time after clearing away breakfast, unless a sweet or some other advance preparation has been seen to the previous evening.

■ Lunch-time entertaining doesn't mean roughing it in the kitchen—so polish up the silver and let your best china see the light of day.

■ Finally, a word of warning: *never* make the mistake of inviting lunch guests too early in the day. For one thing, you'll horrify your bachelor friends, for whom a lunch party is the most delicious prospect imaginable to look forward to at the end of a long, relaxing weekend morning.

Thin envelopes of pounded veal hold a delicious filling of tongue and mushrooms. Recipe page 19.

Avocado, Tomato and Onion Appetizer

4–6 large slices Spanish onion
2 large ripe avocados
6 firm ripe tomatoes
1–2 tablespoons chopped parsley
Finely chopped fresh herbs:
    basil, tarragon or chives

Vinaigrette Dressing
3 tablespoons olive oil
1–2 tablespoons wine vinegar
Salt and freshly ground pepper
Pinch of dry mustard
Pinch of sugar

■ **To make vinaigrette:** beat olive oil and vinegar with a fork; season generously with salt, freshly ground pepper and a pinch each of mustard and sugar. ■ Take onion rings apart and use only those that are between 1½ and 2 inches in diameter. Soak them in iced water for 15 minutes; drain thoroughly. ■ Peel avocados and cut into rings across the width, slipping each ring off the stone as you slice it. ■ Toss avocados with vinaigrette, coating each ring thoroughly to prevent it discolouring. Arrange in a deep serving dish. ■ Slice tomatoes and add them to the avocados, together with onion slices. Toss lightly; sprinkle with chopped parsley and fresh basil, tarragon or chives, to taste, and toss again. ■ Serve very cold.

Serves 6.

A refreshing appetizer of avocado, tomatoes and onions, tossed together with vinaigrette dressing and chopped fresh herbs.

Sauté of Veal with Asparagus

2 lb mature asparagus
Salt
2 lb boned loin of veal
3 oz butter
Freshly ground pepper
4 spring onions or shallots,
   finely chopped
1½ oz flour
¼ pint double cream
1 teaspoon lemon juice

■ Clean asparagus carefully, trimming root ends. Cut stalks in two, separating tips and stems. Cook tips and stems until tender in separate pans of simmering salted water: tips for about 8 minutes, stems 3 to 5 minutes longer. Drain well, reserving cooking liquors; keep hot. ■ Cut veal into 2-inch cubes. ■ Melt butter in a wide, heavy pan or casserole without letting it colour, and sauté veal gently until golden on all sides. Season to taste with salt and freshly ground pepper. ■ Add chopped spring onions or shallots, and sauté for a few minutes longer. ■ Sprinkle veal and onions with flour, and simmer gently until flour is cooked, taking great care as before not to let ingredients brown. ■ Stir in $\frac{3}{4}$ to 1 pint reserved asparagus liquor; cover and simmer for 15 to 20 minutes, or until veal is tender. ■ Purée asparagus tips in a liquidiser or rub through a fine sieve. Stir purée into veal, together with cream and lemon juice. Taste for seasoning, adding more salt, freshly ground pepper or lemon juice if necessary. (Asparagus liquor will already have contributed some salt.) Simmer for 7 to 8 minutes longer. ■ Heat a large, deep serving dish. Transfer veal to the dish and pour over sauce. Arrange asparagus stems attractively in small bunches around sides of dish and serve immediately, accompanied by a bowl of white rice.

tender, with every grain separate. ■ Test rice by biting through a grain: it should be *al dente*, i.e. offering just slight resistance to the tooth, with only a trace of opaque white core remaining in the centre. Untreated long-grain rice will cook in about 18 minutes. ■ Drain rice thoroughly in a colander, and keep hot in a lightly buttered bowl over hot water, covered with a folded cloth to absorb moisture.

Serves 6.

Plain Boiled Rice

■ Bring a large pan of salted water to the boil. When it is bubbling, dribble in 12 oz long-grain rice through your fingers. Stir once or twice to dislodge any grains stuck to the bottom of the pan, and continue to boil gently until rice is

Pineapple Ambrosia

3 small ripe pineapples, about
   1 lb each
2 oranges
2 bananas
Juice of $\frac{1}{2}$ large lemon
$\frac{1}{2}$ lb fresh strawberries
3 oz icing sugar
3 oz freshly grated or
   dessicated coconut

■ Using a very sharp knife, slice each pineapple in half vertically through the flesh and leafy stem. Carefully scoop out flesh, leaving a firm shell; cut flesh into small dice and put it in a bowl. ■ Peel oranges and remove every scrap of pith. Divide oranges into segments and each segment into 3 or 4 pieces, discarding pips. Add to diced pineapple. ■ Hull strawberries; halve or quarter them, depending on size, and toss lightly in the bowl with remaining fruit.
■ Layer fruit in pineapple shells, sifting a little icing sugar to taste between each layer. Sprinkle with coconut and chill until ready to serve.

Pineapple Ambrosia—a simple dessert of fresh fruit in a spectacular presentation.

Pâté Liégeoise

1 lb chicken livers
Salt
8 oz unsalted butter
4 tablespoons grated Spanish
   onion
2 teaspoons dry mustard
$\frac{1}{2}$ teaspoon freshly grated
   nutmeg
$\frac{1}{4}$ teaspoon ground cloves
Freshly ground pepper

■ Cover livers with salted water; bring to the boil; reduce heat and simmer, covered, for 20 minutes. Drain livers, pat dry, and put twice through the finest blade of your mincer—or liquidize in an electric blender. ■ Return paste to pan and beat over a moderate heat for 1 minute to evaporate excess moisture. ■ Work butter with a wooden spoon until soft and creamy. Flavour with onion, mustard, nutmeg and cloves; then beat in minced livers. Season to taste with salt and freshly ground pepper. If you prefer an absolutely smooth texture, rub pâté through a fine sieve. ■ Pack pâté firmly into one or two small earthenware pots or terrines, and chill until ready to serve. Serve with hot toast. ■ Any left over can be kept in the refrigerator for several weeks.

Serves 6.

German Veal with Almonds

6 oz button mushrooms, thinly
   sliced
4 tablespoons butter
4 tablespoons olive oil
Salt and freshly ground pepper
2 tablespoons Madeira
6 veal escalopes, about 4–5 oz
   each
6 oz cooked tongue
1–2 eggs
3 oz fine dry breadcrumbs
2 oz flaked almonds
Plain flour

■ Sauté mushrooms in 1 tablespoon each butter and olive oil until soft and golden. Add salt and freshly ground pepper, to taste; sprinkle with Madeira and allow to cool. ■ Beat escalopes out as thinly as possible. ■ Cut tongue into thin strips; divide into 6 bundles and pile each bundle in the centre of an escalope. Spoon mushrooms over the top and fold each escalope into an envelope. ■ Beat egg(s) lightly with a little water. Toss breadcrumbs with flaked almonds. ■ Dust veal "envelopes" with flour; dip into beaten egg and coat with almond-breadcrumb mixture, patting it on firmly. Chill. ■ **To cook veal:** melt remaining butter and oil, and fry veal "envelopes" slowly on both sides until golden brown, about 10 minutes. Serve immediately with a sauceboat of Quick Hollandaise Sauce (overleaf).

Serves 6.

Quick Hollandaise Sauce

6 oz butter
6 egg yolks
Lemon juice
Salt and white pepper

■ Melt butter in a small pan, taking care that it does not bubble or sizzle. ■ Warm goblet of an electric blender and in it combine egg yolks with $1\frac{1}{2}$ teaspoons lemon juice, $1\frac{1}{2}$ tablespoons water, and a pinch each of salt and white pepper. ■ Switch blender to moderate speed and, when yolks are well mixed, remove lid and pour in butter in a thin stream. If butter is poured in slowly enough, sauce will thicken into a genuine Hollandaise.

However, if it remains too liquid, transfer to the top of a double saucepan and stir over hot water for a few seconds to thicken it; conversely, an over-stiff sauce may be thinned by beating in a tablespoon or two of very hot water. ■ Add more salt, pepper or lemon juice, if necessary, and keep sauce warm over *warm* water.

Serves 6.

Gratin Dauphinois

2 lb potatoes
1 pint milk
Salt and freshly ground pepper
4 tablespoons butter
$\frac{1}{2}$ pint single cream
8 tablespoons grated Gruyère
3 tablespoons grated Parmesan

Menu II

■ Preheat oven to moderate (375°F. Mark 5). ■ Peel and slice potatoes thinly into a bowl of cold water. Soak for a few minutes; then drain slices thoroughly and arrange in a 2-pint gratin dish. ■ Pour over milk; season to taste with salt and freshly ground pepper. ■ Bake for 20 to 30 minutes, or until potatoes are half-cooked. Remove from oven and reduce temperature to 325°F. (Mark 3). ■ Drain potatoes. Rinse and dry gratin dish, and grease it with 2 tablespoons butter. ■ Layer potato slices in buttered dish. Pour over cream; sprinkle with grated cheeses and dot with remaining butter. ■ Return to the oven for a further 30 minutes, or until potatoes are tender, with a bubbling, golden crust. (Cover dish with foil if they brown too quickly.) Serve very hot.

Serves 6.

Green Bean Salad

Boil 1½ lb French beans in salted water for 5 to 8 minutes until just cooked. Drain. ■ Toss while still hot with a vinaigrette dressing to which you have added 1 to 2 tablespoons *very* finely chopped onion, 3 to 4 tablespoons chopped parsley and a teaspoon of chopped fresh tarragon. ■ Serve cold, following the main course.

Serves 6.

Fresh Blackcurrant Sorbet

1½ lb trimmed blackcurrants
9 oz sugar
1 tablespoon lemon juice
3 egg whites
Raspberry purée, to serve
  (see method)

■ Turn refrigerator to its highest setting, i.e. lowest temperature.
■ Put blackcurrants in the top of a double saucepan with 9 tablespoons water. Cook over simmering water for 30 minutes, or until blackcurrants have released their juice. Strain through a fine sieve, pressing out as much juice as possible with the back of a spoon. ■ Dissolve sugar in ¾ pint water and simmer for 10 minutes. Stir in lemon juice.
■ Combine sugar syrup with blackcurrant juice in a measuring jug. Make up to 1½ pints with water. Taste mixture and if it seems too sharp, add a little more water. (Remember, however, that the addition of egg whites later will modify flavour, as will freezing itself.) ■ Pour mixture into an oiled freezer tray or loaf tin and freeze until half set, about 1 hour.
■ Remove from refrigerator and stir well with a fork to break up ice crystals. ■ Beat egg whites until stiff but not dry, and fold gently but thoroughly into sorbet. ■ Freeze until firm, stirring once or twice with a fork to ensure that sorbet does not separate. ■ Serve with a bowl of raspberry purée—fresh raspberries rubbed through a fine sieve and flavoured to taste with a little icing sugar and lemon juice.

Serves 6.

Caesar Salad with Mushrooms

2 cloves garlic
$\frac{1}{4}$ pint olive oil
2 small heads Cos lettuce
8 oz small white button
   mushrooms
4 tablespoons lemon juice
2 eggs
$\frac{1}{2}$ teaspoon salt
$\frac{1}{4}$ teaspoon dry mustard
$\frac{1}{4}$ teaspoon freshly ground
   pepper
3–4 slices white bread, $\frac{1}{4}$ inch
   thick
4 anchovy fillets, finely chopped
   (optional)
8 tablespoons freshly grated
   Parmesan

■ Peel and crush garlic cloves lightly. Let them steep in olive oil for 2 hours so that oil becomes impregnated with their flavour. Then strain oil through a fine sieve and discard garlic. ■ Wash lettuce and pat each leaf dry individually in a clean cloth. (This is important, as the dressing must not be diluted with water from the leaves.) Break leaves into a salad bowl in fairly large pieces. ■ Clean and trim mushrooms, and slice thinly. Toss thoroughly with lemon juice to preserve colour. ■ Drop eggs into boiling water; simmer for just 90 seconds and drain immediately. (This is known as "coddling".) ■ In a small bowl, combine salt with dry mustard and freshly ground pepper. Drain off lemon juice from mushrooms and blend with seasonings; then beat in 6 tablespoons of the garlic-flavoured oil to make a dressing. ■ Cut bread into $\frac{1}{4}$-inch cubes. ■ Heat

remaining garlic oil in a frying pan; add bread cubes and toss over a moderate heat until crisp and golden, adding a little more olive oil if necessary. Drain well on absorbent paper. ■ Just before serving: pour dressing over lettuce; add finely chopped anchovies, if used, and toss well. ■ When leaves are thoroughly coated with dressing, break coddled eggs into the centre and toss again. ■ Finally, add sliced mushrooms, garlic croûtons and grated Parmesan; toss lightly but thoroughly so that no excess dressing remains at the bottom of the bowl, and serve immediately.

Serves 6.

The great American Caesar Salad: crisp leaves of Cos lettuce bathed in a creamy dressing flavoured with garlic and freshly grated Parmesan, and tossed at the table with garlic croûtons. In this version we add sliced raw mushrooms to the traditional recipe.

Roast Chicken with Almonds and Herbed Rice

A 4- to 4½-lb roasting chicken
3 oz seedless raisins
4–5 oz butter
Salt and freshly ground pepper
1 chicken liver
4–5 tablespoons corn oil
1 large Spanish onion or
  2 medium-sized onions, finely
  chopped
12 oz long-grain rice
1½ chicken stock cubes
1 teaspoon dried thyme
3 oz flaked almonds

■ Soak raisins in warm water to plump them up. ■ Preheat oven to moderately hot (400°F. Mark 6).

Menu III

Season 2 to 3 tablespoons of the butter with salt and freshly ground pepper, kneading it thoroughly with your fingertips. Divide seasoned butter in half, flatten it out slightly and slip a piece right down between the skin and meat of each chicken breast, loosening skin away from breast gently with your fingers. ■ Season bird inside with salt and freshly ground pepper; add chicken liver and 2 tablespoons butter. Rub outside of chicken generously with salt and freshly ground pepper, and spread with remaining butter. ■ Roast chicken for 1 to $1\frac{1}{4}$ hours, or until tender and crisp, turning it occasionally. Halfway through cooking time, baste with 2 to 3 tablespoons boiling water.

Meanwhile, prepare rice: heat oil in a large, heavy saucepan.

Roast Chicken served on a bed of herbed rice, and garnished with almonds and raisins.

Add finely chopped onion and sauté gently until soft and golden. Stir in rice and continue to sauté gently, stirring, until each grain is separate and golden. ■ Dissolve chicken stock cubes in $1\frac{1}{4}$ pints boiling water. ■ Remove rice from heat and stir in stock and dried thyme. Cover and simmer very gently for about 15 minutes, or until rice is tender and fluffy, but not overcooked, and all the liquid has been absorbed. Stir gently with a fork two or three times while rice is cooking. (If necessary, it can be kept in a buttered bowl covered with a folded cloth over a saucepan of hot water until chicken is ready.)

■ Arrange rice on a heated serving dish. Place well-drained, roasted chicken on top and keep hot while you finish sauce. ■ Transfer roasting tin with buttery chicken juices to top of stove. Add flaked almonds and sauté until a deep golden colour, stirring constantly.

Remove almonds from tin with a slotted spoon and keep hot. ■ Drain raisins thoroughly and add them to the roasting tin with 2 to 3 tablespoons boiling water. Simmer for about 2 minutes, scraping bottom and sides of pan with a wooden spoon. Season to taste with more salt and freshly ground pepper if necessary, and spoon buttery sauce over chicken and rice. ■ Sprinkle with sautéed almonds and serve immediately.

Serves 6.

Bread and Butter Pudding à l'Orange

4–6 oz softened butter
10–12 slices thick-cut white
   bread
4 tablespoons marmalade
Juice and finely grated rind of
   2 large oranges and 1 lemon
3 oz castor sugar

Custard
¾ pint milk
2 eggs
2 tablespoons castor sugar
1 oz seedless raisins (optional)
4 tablespoons lightly whipped
   cream

Menu III

■ Preheat oven to moderately hot (400°F. Mark 6). Grease a shallow 3-pint baking dish generously with some of the butter. ■ Remove crusts from bread. Spread slices with butter and marmalade, and cut into triangles (4 to each slice).
■ Combine juice and finely grated rinds of oranges and lemon in a bowl. Add castor sugar and stir until melted. ■ Line bottom and sides of prepared baking dish completely with bread triangles, soaking them in orange syrup and arranging them buttered side up. Fill lined dish with some of remaining triangles, reserving a few to decorate top of pudding.
■ **To make custard :** heat milk to just below boiling point. Beat eggs lightly and pour hot milk on them gradually, beating constantly. Return mixture to pan; add sugar, and raisins, if used, and stir over a low heat until custard thickens enough to coat back of spoon, taking great care not to let it boil, or eggs will curdle. (Use a double saucepan if available.) ■ Remove custard from heat; cool slightly and stir in cream. ■ Pour custard over bread in the baking dish. ■ Cut remaining bread triangles in half; soak each one in remaining orange syrup and arrange them on top in an attractive pattern. Sprinkle with any left-over orange syrup. ■ Bake pudding for 30 minutes, or until crisp and golden on the outside, with a soft, creamy centre.

Serves 6.

Salade de Moules au Kari

8 oz long-grain rice
Salt
3 pints mussels
½ pint dry white wine
1 onion, finely chopped
2 level teaspoons curry powder
4 oz peeled shrimps
2 firm tomatoes, sliced
1–2 tablespoons chopped parsley
Crisp lettuce leaves, to garnish

Vinaigrette Dressing
1 shallot, finely chopped
2 tablespoons wine vinegar
5 tablespoons olive oil
Salt and freshly ground pepper

■ Boil rice in salted water until tender but still firm. Drain thoroughly; cool. ■ Scrub mussels clean and remove "beards". Place them in a heavy pan with wine, chopped onion and curry powder; cover tightly and cook over a high heat, shaking pan frequently, until mussels have all opened, 5 to 7 minutes. ■ Shell mussels over pan to catch any liquor trapped inside. ■ Filter liquor through muslin and return to rinsed-out pan; add shrimps and simmer for 15 minutes. ■ Drain shrimps, reserving liquor, and combine with rice and mussels in a bowl. ■ Add sliced tomatoes and chopped parsley. ■ Simmer shrimp liquor until reduced to about 3 tablespoons. ■ Make a highly seasoned vinaigrette, beating with a fork until ingredients form an emulsion. Blend in reduced shrimp liquor. ■ Pour over salad; toss lightly and chill before serving. ■ Serve salad piled in a lettuce-lined bowl.

Serves 6.

Shepherd's Pie

Butter
1 Spanish onion, finely chopped
2 tablespoons olive oil
1 lb cooked roast beef,
  coarsely minced
$\frac{1}{2}$ pint rich beef gravy or Quick
  Brown Sauce (see overleaf)
2 teaspoons Worcester sauce
1 tablespoon chopped parsley
$\frac{1}{4}$ teaspoon mixed herbs
Salt and freshly ground pepper

Potato topping
6 tablespoons double cream
3 tablespoons melted butter
2 eggs, lightly beaten
2 lb potatoes, peeled, boiled
  and mashed
Salt and freshly ground pepper

■ Generously butter a deep, 3-pint baking dish. ■ Preheat oven to moderately hot (400°F. Mark 6). ■ Sauté chopped onion in olive oil until soft and transparent. Stir in minced cooked beef, gravy or Quick Brown Sauce, Worcester sauce, chopped parsley and mixed herbs, and season to taste with salt and freshly ground pepper. Remove from heat. ■ **To make potato topping:** beat cream, 2 tablespoons melted butter and the lightly beaten eggs into hot mashed potatoes, and season to taste with salt and freshly ground pepper. ■ Spread meat mixture evenly in baking dish. Top with mashed potatoes and brush with remaining melted butter. ■ Bake for 20 to 25 minutes, or until potatoes are puffed and golden brown.

Serves 6.

Quick Brown Sauce

■ Melt 2 tablespoons butter in a heavy pan. Add 1 Spanish onion and a medium-sized carrot, both roughly chopped, ½ bay leaf, 3 stalks parsley and a sprig of fresh thyme or a pinch of dried thyme. Brown vegetables thoroughly, stirring occasionally with a wooden spoon and scraping bottom of pan. Dust with 2 tablespoons flour and continue to cook until this has browned as well. ■ Stir in 1 teaspoon tomato purée and a beef stock cube dissolved in ¾ pint hot water, scraping bottom of pan

vigorously to dislodge crusty brown bits stuck there. Season lightly with freshly ground pepper and simmer for 45 minutes, stirring occasionally. ■ Strain sauce through a fine sieve, pressing vegetables against sides of sieve to extract all their juices. Correct seasoning. ■ The sauce can be used immediately, or stored for 2 days in an airtight container in the refrigerator.

An informal family lunch of Shepherd's Pie served with Sautéed Courgettes in a ring of chopped onion and tomato.

Sautéed Courgettes

12 courgettes
Salt
6 tablespoons flour
6 tablespoons freshly grated
   Parmesan
Freshly ground pepper
4 tablespoons olive oil
4 tablespoons butter
1 Spanish onion, coarsely
   chopped
6 tomatoes, peeled, seeded and
   chopped

■ Poach courgettes in boiling salted water until just tender, 5 to 8 minutes. Drain thoroughly and slice thickly. ■ Combine flour with freshly grated Parmesan and season with salt and freshly ground pepper. Toss courgette slices in this mixture until lightly coated. ■ Heat oil in a heavy sauté pan and fry courgettes over a moderate heat until golden brown on all sides. Remove from pan with a slotted spoon; drain thoroughly on absorbent paper and keep hot. ■ Melt butter in another heavy pan and sauté coarsely chopped onion until soft and transparent. Add chopped tomatoes and simmer for 2 to 3 minutes longer. ■ Pile courgettes in the centre of a heated serving dish and surround with sautéed onion and tomatoes. Serve hot.

Serves 6.

Cold Lemon Soufflé

3 eggs, separated
5 oz castor sugar
Finely grated rind and strained
   juice of 3 large lemons
2 teaspoons powdered gelatine
½ pint double cream
Whipped cream, to decorate
   (optional)

■ Tie a double thickness of greaseproof paper around the outside of a 5-inch soufflé dish to come at least 2 inches above the rim. ■ Place egg yolks in a bowl; add sugar and whisk over hot water until very light, white and fluffy. ■ Gradually add grated lemon rind and strained juice, beating constantly, and whisk until mixture thickens; then remove from heat and whisk until cool. ■ In a small cup, soften gelatine in 3 to 4 tablespoons cold water; place cup in a pan of hot water and stir gently until gelatine has completely dissolved. ■ Whisk egg whites until stiff but not dry. ■ Whisk cream until barely stiff enough to hold its shape. ■ Whisk dissolved gelatine into egg and lemon mixture (for a completely smooth texture, they should both ideally be at the same temperature). Carefully fold in cream, followed by beaten egg whites. ■ Pour mixture into prepared soufflé dish and chill until set. ■ To serve: carefully peel off paper collar from dish and serve soufflé decorated with more piped whipped cream if liked.
■ Accompany by a plate of crisp *langues de chat (*see overleaf).

Serves 6.

Langues de Chat

Butter and flour for baking
  sheets
2 oz softened butter
2 oz castor sugar
2 egg whites
2 oz plain flour

■ Preheat oven to fairly hot
(425°F. Mark 7). Butter and dust
2 or 3 baking sheets with flour,
shaking off excess. ■ In a small
bowl, beat softened butter until
creamy. Add sugar and beat
vigorously with a wooden spoon
until mixture is very pale and fluffy
again. (This will take several
minutes and the success of the
biscuits largely depends on adequate
beating.) ■ Put egg whites in a
shallow dish. Then, with a teaspoon,
add them (unbeaten) to the butter
mixture a little at a time, beating
vigorously between each addition.
■ Sift flour over mixture and fold in
lightly but thoroughly with a metal
spoon. ■ Spoon mixture into a
piping bag fitted with a plain
$\frac{1}{4}$-inch nozzle and pipe out in 3-inch
lengths, spacing them about
2 inches apart, as they spread
considerably. If you do not have
enough baking sheets to take all the
biscuits at once, the mixture will
come to no harm if piped out and
baked in batches. ■ Bake for 5
minutes, or until biscuits are very
thin and tinged with brown round
the edges. ■ Quickly transfer to
wire cooling racks with a spatula
and allow to become quite cold and
crisp before storing in an airtight
container.

Makes about 24.

Crab Louis with Cucumber

½ pint well-flavoured, home-made
   mayonnaise
2 tablespoons tomato ketchup
3 tablespoons olive oil
1 tablespoon wine vinegar
2 tablespoons grated onion
2 tablespoons finely chopped
   parsley
6 tablespoons double cream,
   whipped
Tabasco or Worcester sauce
   (optional)
Salt and freshly ground pepper
Cayenne pepper
1–2 tablespoons chopped stuffed
   or ripe pitted olives
1 lb cooked crabmeat, flaked
Thinly sliced unpeeled cucumber,
   lettuce leaves and
   2 tablespoons chopped
   chives, to garnish

■ Blend first 7 ingredients together.
Season with Tabasco or Worcester
sauce, if used, salt, freshly ground
pepper and a dash of cayenne, to
taste. ■ Stir in chopped olives and
chill for at least 1 hour, preferably 2,
before serving. ■ When ready to
serve, fold flaked crabmeat into
sauce. ■ Decorate outer edge of
4 or 6 individual plates with a ring
of overlapping cucumber slices, and
lay a large, crisp lettuce leaf in the
centre. Pile with crabmeat mixture
and serve, garnished with chopped
chives.

Serves 4–6.

"Tournedos" of Lamb

1 Spanish onion
1 clove garlic
2 tablespoons butter
2 tablespoons olive oil
2 oz soft white breadcrumbs
3–4 tablespoons cold milk
1¼ lb lean minced lamb
3 tablespoons chopped parsley
¼ teaspoon dried oregano
2 teaspoons Worcester sauce
1 egg
Salt and freshly ground pepper
Flour
6–8 slices fat bacon

■ Finely chop onion and garlic. Simmer them in half the butter and oil until soft; cool. Soak breadcrumbs in milk; then squeeze out excess moisture. ■ Place lamb in a large bowl. Add onion, breadcrumbs, herbs, Worcester sauce and egg, and mix well. Season generously with salt and freshly ground pepper. ■ Divide mixture into 6 portions. Shape into balls; roll in flour and flatten into patties 2 inches in diameter. ■ Stretch each bacon slice thinly with the back of a knife to meet round the middle of a patty, making up difference with an extra strip of bacon if necessary, and tie securely with string. ■ Heat remaining fats in a large frying pan, or 2 smaller pans, and fry patties slowly on all sides until cooked through, about 30 minutes. ■ To serve: discard strings; transfer patties to a heated serving dish and serve very hot.

Serves 6.

Potatoes O'Brien

2–2½ lb potatoes
1 large green pepper
1 large Spanish onion
1 tablespoon flour
4 tablespoons chopped parsley
4 oz freshly grated cheese
Pinch of cayenne
Salt and freshly ground pepper
¼ pint hot milk
¼ pint double cream
2 tablespoons butter

■ Preheat oven to moderately hot (400°F. Mark 6). ■ Peel potatoes and cut them into ¼-inch dice. Place them in a bowl. ■ Slice pepper in half; remove core and seeds, and chop flesh finely. Add to potatoes. ■ Peel and chop onion finely; toss lightly with diced potatoes and pepper. ■ Sprinkle vegetables with flour, chopped parsley and grated cheese, and toss again. Then season to taste with a pinch of cayenne, salt and a little freshly ground pepper, bearing in mind that the mixture may already be quite peppery because of the green pepper. ■ Spread potato mixture evenly in a 3-pint, ovenproof dish; pour over milk and cream; dot with butter and bake for 1 hour, or until potatoes are soft, with a crisp, golden brown topping.

Serves 6.

Angel Food Cake with Orange Sauce

3 oz plain flour
1 oz cornflour
$\frac{1}{2}$ level teaspoon salt
8 oz castor sugar
10 egg whites
1 tablespoon lemon juice
1 level teaspoon cream of tartar
$\frac{1}{2}$ teaspoon vanilla essence

■ Preheat oven to moderate (350°F. Mark 4). ■ Prepare a 9-inch tube cake tin, making sure that it is spotlessly clean, as otherwise the delicate cake will not rise properly. ■ Sift flour with cornflour and salt. Sift castor sugar separately. Then resift flour mixture 3 times with 3 oz of the sugar. ■ Mix egg whites with lemon juice and 1 tablespoon water; beat until foamy. Add cream of tartar and continue to beat until stiff but not dry. ■ Beat in remaining 5 oz castor sugar, a tablespoon at a time. (*Note:* If you are using an electric mixer, start adding sugar a little earlier to avoid overbeating.) ■ Flavour with vanilla. ■ Sift 2 to 3 tablespoons flour mixture over egg whites and fold in quickly and gently but thoroughly. Fold in remaining flour mixture gradually in the same way. ■ Turn mixture into prepared tin; bake for about 45 minutes, or until cake springs back when lightly pressed with a finger. ■ Remove cake from oven and

Angel Food Cake with Orange Sauce makes the perfect light luncheon finale.

immediately invert tin at an angle, upside down, so that the cake hangs free—a milk bottle is good for this. Leave cake hanging for about 1½ hours, or until quite set and cold. ■ Then gently shake cake out of the tin on to a serving dish. Serve with orange sauce (see below).

Orange Sauce

Juice of 4 large oranges and
  ½ lemon
Finely grated rind of 2 oranges
2 tablespoons arrowroot
3 tablespoons castor sugar
2 tablespoons butter
2 egg yolks, lightly beaten
1–2 teaspoons Grand Marnier

■ Combine orange and lemon juice with grated orange rind in a measuring jug. There should be ½ pint liquid. Make up to 1 pint with water. ■ Mix arrowroot smoothly with some of juice; then combine with remaining juice and pour into a pan. ■ Bring to the boil, stirring, and simmer for 2 to 3 minutes, until sauce is thick and translucent. ■ Beat in sugar and butter over a low heat until dissolved. ■ Pour hot sauce over lightly beaten egg yolks, beating constantly. ■ Return to pan and stir over a low heat for a minute or two longer until sauce thickens slightly, taking great care not to let it boil. ■ Strain sauce; cool slightly and flavour to taste with a little Grand Marnier. ■ Serve warm or cool.

Smoked Trout Appetizer

3 smoked trout
6 slices white bread
6 tablespoons double cream
1–2 tablespoons grated
   horseradish, or to taste
Finely chopped parsley

Garnish
6 crisp lettuce leaves
6 slices firm tomato
6 large black olives, pitted and
   halved
6 lemon wedges

■ Skin and fillet smoked trout, and cut each fillet in two. ■ Toast bread slices on both sides and remove crusts. ■ Whisk double cream; add 1 to 2 tablespoons iced water and whisk again until firm. Fold in grated horseradish, to taste. ■ Spread each slice of toast with horseradish chantilly cream and arrange 4 pieces of trout on top. Sprinkle with a pinch of finely chopped parsley. Cut each slice of toast in half diagonally. ■ Serve 2 toast triangles per person on individual plates garnished with lettuce, tomato, black olives, and lemon wedges to squeeze over the trout.

Serves 6.

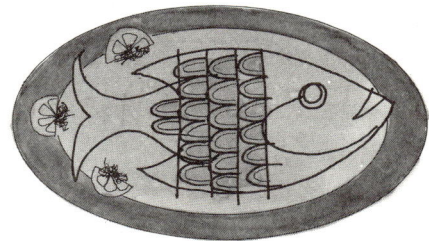

Omelette Arlésienne

A rich, thick omelette which makes a substantial summer luncheon dish. Follow with a fresh green salad.

3 ripe aubergines
Salt
8 tablespoons olive oil
1 Spanish onion, finely chopped
2 lb ripe tomatoes, peeled,
   seeded and diced
Freshly ground pepper
1 clove garlic, finely chopped
4 tablespoons finely chopped
   parsley
8 eggs
1–2 tablespoons melted butter

■ Peel aubergines and cut flesh into dice. Leave them to soak in a bowl of salted water for at least $\frac{1}{2}$ hour.
■ Heat half the olive oil in a deep, heavy frying pan. Add finely chopped onion and diced tomatoes, and sauté gently for a few minutes.
■ Drain aubergines thoroughly, squeezing out as much as possible of their bitter juices between the palms of your hands. Add aubergines to the simmering tomato mixture and mix well. ■ Season to taste with salt and freshly ground pepper, and cook gently for about 25 minutes, stirring occasionally

Above, left: *Preparing vegetable garnish for Omelette Arlésienne*
Above, right: *Filling the omelette*
Below: *Omelette Arlésienne*

with a wooden spoon. ■ Add finely chopped garlic and parsley, mix well and cook for a minute longer. Remove from heat and keep warm. ■ Beat eggs lightly with a fork. Season to taste with salt and freshly ground pepper. ■ Heat remaining oil in a large omelette pan; pour in eggs and stir over a moderate heat until they begin to thicken and have set underneath. ■ Spoon aubergine mixture down centre, reserving 2 or 3 tablespoons for garnish. ■ Continue to cook omelette until firm and golden brown on the underside but still creamy on top; then slide it up one side of the pan and fold it over on itself. ■ Slip folded omelette out carefully on to a heated serving dish. Brush with melted butter and garnish with remaining aubergine mixture. Serve immediately.

Serves 4–6.

Grapefruit Mint Salad

1 round lettuce
1 Cos lettuce
2 grapefruit
2 teaspoons lemon juice
5 tablespoons olive oil
Salt and freshly ground pepper
6 leaves fresh mint, finely
   chopped

■ Wash lettuce carefully. Pat each leaf dry individually and store in the chilling compartment of the refrigerator, rolled up in a clean cloth, until needed. ■ With a sharp knife, peel grapefruit, slicing off bitter pith and membranes together with the skin, and catching juices in a small bowl. Cut segments out of membranes; then squeeze membranes into the dish. ■ Combine grapefruit juice with lemon juice; add olive oil and beat with a fork until mixture emulsifies. Season to taste with salt and freshly ground pepper, and stir in finely chopped mint. ■ Just before serving: break lettuce leaves into a salad bowl. Pour over dressing and toss thoroughly. ■ Finally, add grapefruit segments; toss again and serve immediately.

Serves 6.

Rhubarb Pie

8 oz shortcrust pastry
2 eggs
Castor sugar
$\frac{1}{4}$ teaspoon salt
Finely grated rind of 1 orange
1 oz plain flour
2 lb forced rhubarb, trimmed
    and cut into $1\frac{1}{2}$-inch lengths
1 tablespoon butter
1 egg yolk, beaten with 1
    tablespoon milk

■ Preheat oven to hot (450°F. Mark 8). ■ Line a 9-inch pie dish with pastry, reserving enough to make a lattice of wide strips over top of pie. ■ Beat eggs until fluffy. Gradually add 10 oz castor sugar, the salt and finely grated orange rind, beating constantly. Sift flour over the top and fold in thoroughly.

Menu VI

■ Combine prepared rhubarb with egg and sugar mixture. Pour into lined pie dish and dot with butter. ■ Roll remaining pastry out thinly and cut into strips about ½ inch wide with a fluted pastry wheel. Lay strips in a lattice over top of pie. Brush pastry with egg yolk beaten with milk. ■ Bake pie for 15 minutes; then reduce temperature to 350°F. (Mark 4) and bake for a further 30 minutes. ■ Dust top of pie with a little castor sugar and serve hot or lukewarm, with cream if liked.

Serves 6.

Note: As the rhubarb season advances, you will probably find that (*a*) pie requires less sugar, say 8 oz; and (*b*) thicker stems mean that you have to cut them into shorter lengths.

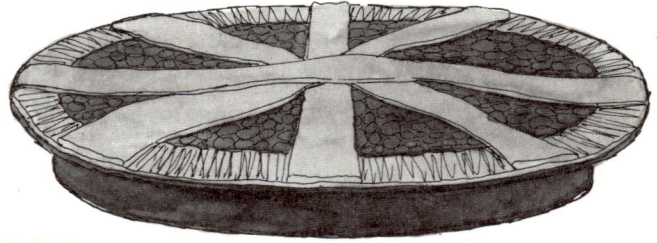